First published in Great
Britain in 2001 by Zero To Ten Limited
327 High Street, Slough, Berkshire, SL1 1TX

Publisher: Anna McQuinn
Art Director: Tim Foster
Senior Editor: Simona Sideri
Publishing Assistant: Vikram Parashar

A CIP catalogue record for this book is available from
the British Library.
ISBN 1-84089-082-7
Printed in Hong Kong

Imagine you're a Pirate!

Peg Leg Meg

Meg gave up being a pirate two years ago and
now lives the life of a landlubber with her husband,
John. She has a gypsy caravan where she writes about
the secrets of the sea and a dog whom she is training
to look for treasure but so far he has only found bones.
She tries to follow the pirates' code but finds it
very difficult (especially rule no.6).

Lucy Blackheart

Lucy lives in an enchanting faraway land where
she paints pictures about her favourite things.
She has often imagined having exciting adventures and
discovering treasure islands and meeting mermaids.
However, she would much rather stay at home painting
about the life of a pirate than suffer the hardships of
being a real one herself.

We dedicate this book to Simona – a real treasure!

What is a pirate?

Definition:
a robber who attacks
other ships at sea.

What do pirates look like?

There are some pirates who are big and strong and bold.

There are some pirates who are tall and thin and cunning.

Pirates can come in many different shapes and sizes but...
all pirates are very, very wicked.

Becoming a pirate

You can become a pirate by running away from home with all your things tied up in a spotty hanky. You have to walk to the nearest port and become a cabin boy or girl on a pirate ship. Then you have to learn how to be very, very wicked. This takes a long time and gets a bit boring after a while, so most people prefer to stay at home and watch a bit of television with a delicious supper!

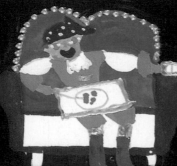

The Pirate Code

1 Never be kind to children (especially the cabin boy or girl).
2 Never be kind to mermaids.
3 Never be kind to anyone.
4 Always look fierce.
5 Always carry a cutlass.
6 Always obey the captain.

The pirate motto:

Rob or rot!

What do pirates wear?

Equipment and accessories

In order to be a pirate you will need some of the following equipment...

Spotty hanky

Eye patch

Earrings

Three-cornered hat with gold braid

Spade

Cutlass

Dagger

Stick on Tattoos

Wooden leg or hook

Scrubbing brush

Parrot

Bottle of grog

Where do pirates work?

Pirates sail the Seven Seas looking for ships to rob.
Nobody really knows where the Seven Seas are.
There are several oceans: Pacific, Atlantic, Arctic, Indian
and Antarctic, and many seas, such as the Irish Sea,
the Caribbean, the Mediterranean and the China Sea,
but only pirates can find the Seven Seas.

The Seven Seas have mermaids and sunken vessels
and coral reefs and treasure islands, but you have to be
a pirate to get there.
At the bottom of the Seven Seas is something called
Davy Jones' locker. Pirates say that when they die or
get killed and are thrown overboard they float
down to Davy Jones' locker and live
with the mermaids.

$\mathfrak{S}$cattered around the Seven Seas are
many treasure islands. When the pirates have worked out
which one is which they set sail. This is not always very easy
because they encounter various difficulties on the way such as
sea monsters, typhoons, marauding buccaneers or mutineers on
board ship and they often run out of grog.
The only thing that keeps them going is the hope that they might
meet some friendly mermaids. Mermaids have bodies like women
and tails like fish and they comb their seaweed-green hair
with shells.

They are very beautiful but not very reliable and sometimes
end up putting the pirates off their job of searching for treasure.
Eventually the pirates find the treasure islands and the treasure.
Treasure is always jewels, or pieces of eight, or dubloons,
or Spanish gold, and it is kept in big treasure chests buried
in sand or caverns.

You always know which is a pirate ship because it will be flying the pirates' flag called the **'Jolly Roger'**. It is a black flag with a white skull and crossed thigh bones on it, sometimes known as the skull and crossbones. When you see this flag you get very, very frightened.

Pirates never buy their own ships. They always steal other people's ships so they often have pretty names such as...

Saucy ◆ Sue

Lovely Lady

PRETTY PEGGY

 Hispaniola

The ship and her captain

Imagine you are the captain of a real pirate ship. Think of a really wicked name for the ship and then draw a picture of what you'd like her to look like.

The only friends that pirates really have are parrots because they sit on their shoulders and say funny things like 'Who's a pretty boy then?'

Black Revenge

Food and drink

Pirates are at sea for most of the time so they cannot get very much fresh food. They do not get enough vitamins so they get spots and scurvy. Scurvy is a nasty disease you get when you don't eat the right sort of food.

They eat lots of fish.

They eat lots of ship's biscuits which get very maggoty.

They also drink lots of rum, or grog, which they like better than the water kept in barrels on deck.

WATER

WATER

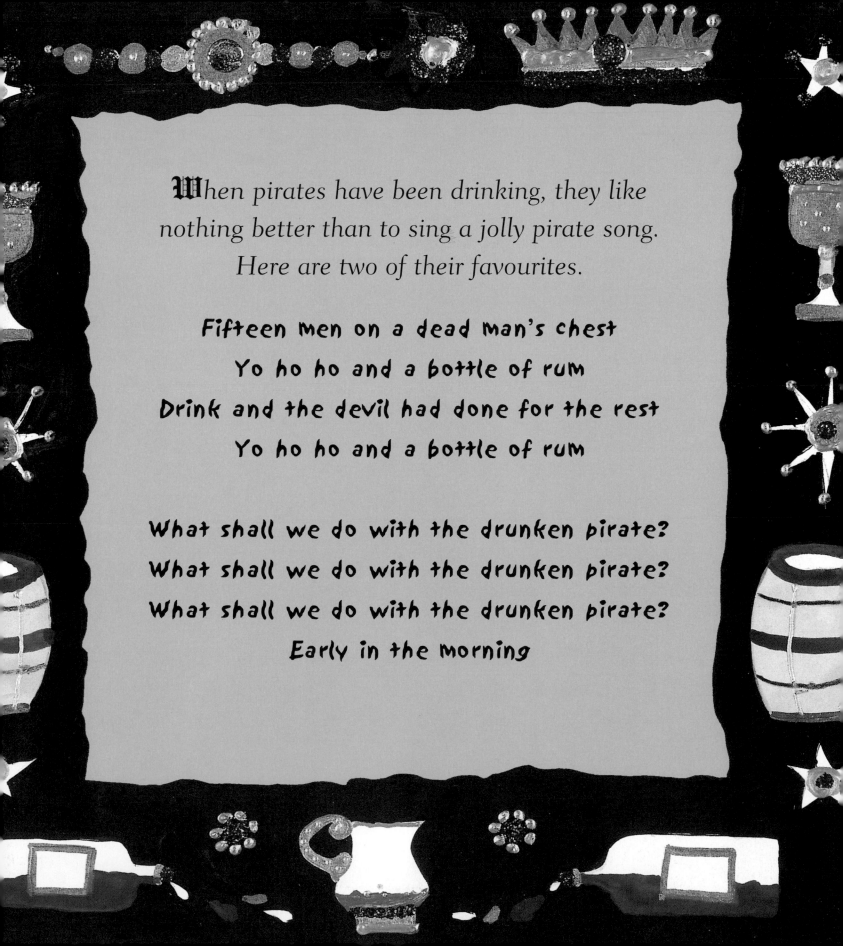

When pirates have been drinking, they like nothing better than to sing a jolly pirate song. Here are two of their favourites.

Fifteen men on a dead man's chest
Yo ho ho and a bottle of rum
Drink and the devil had done for the rest
Yo ho ho and a bottle of rum

What shall we do with the drunken pirate?
What shall we do with the drunken pirate?
What shall we do with the drunken pirate?
Early in the morning

Pirates behaving badly

When pirates disobey the pirate captain they can be cruelly punished in a number of ways...

Flogging

The Captain ties them to the mast and hits them with a nasty whip with long strands called a cat o' nine tails until they are very sorry. Then he throws salt water onto their wounds. Oh dear!

Scrubbing the deck

(This is the worst punishment.) They have to pull up a bucket of salty water from the sea, get down on hands and knees with a scrubbing brush and scrub the entire deck with a constant circular motion until it is clean. Oh dear! Oh dear!

Oh dear! Oh help!

Walking the plank

When pirates capture other ships they sometimes make their captives walk the plank. They tie a plank to the deck so that it sticks out over the sea. Then they make their victims walk to the end so that they fall in –
SPLASH!

Wanted
Black Hearted Bill
For evil deeds on the High Seas
Description: Black greasy hair, dirty teeth,
snarling lips, scar on chin, black moustache
Beware
Do not approach this pirate

Pirate language

 Yo, ho, ho, the frisky plank...

 Ready about skipper.

 Pieces of eight...

 All hands on deck.

 Avast there!

 Splice the mainbrace.

Land ahoy!

 Man overboard!

 Look astern, matey.

 Aye, aye, cap'n!

 Stand by to go about.

 Shiver me timbers!

Pirate words

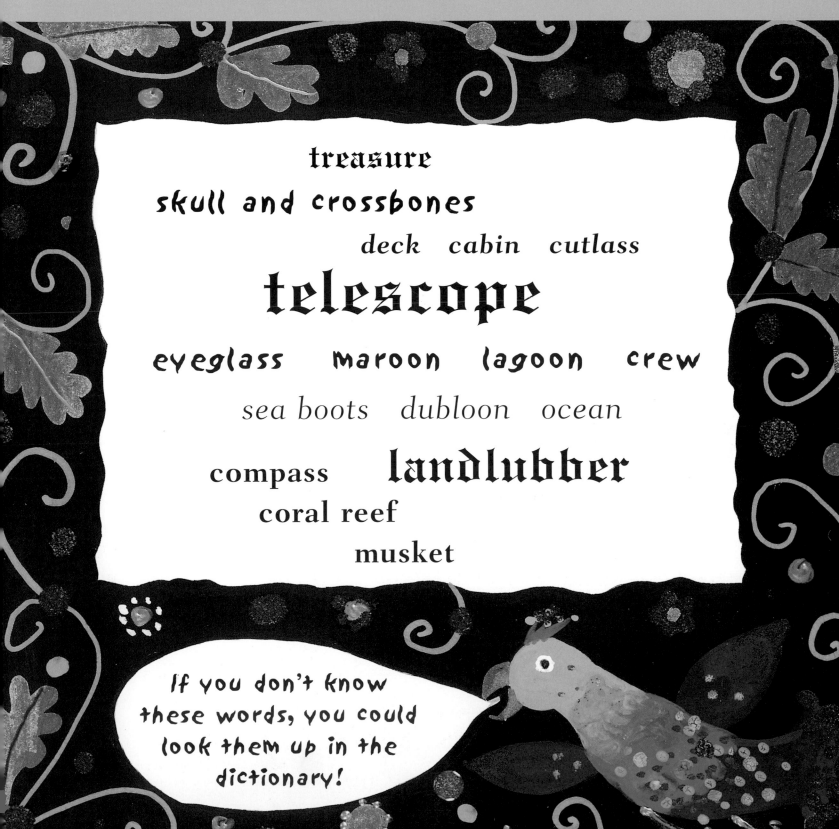

treasure

skull and crossbones

deck   cabin   cutlass

telescope

eyeglass   maroon   lagoon   crew

sea boots   dubloon   ocean

compass   landlubber

coral reef

musket

If you don't know these words, you could look them up in the dictionary!

Captain Hook

Captain Hook is the pirate in J.M. Barrie's book, Peter Pan.
He had a hook because Peter Pan chopped off his hand with
a sword during a fight.

A passing crocodile had eaten the hand and found it to be
so delicious that from then on he chased after Captain Hook
in order to eat the rest of him. Fortunately he had also
swallowed an alarm clock so Captain Hook always knew
when the crocodile was coming.

Tick-tock

Long John Silver

Long John Silver is the pirate in Treasure Island by
R.L. Stevenson. He pretended to be an honest man on board
a ship called the Hispaniola which was searching for treasure,
but really he was the head of a pirate gang who were after
the treasure for themselves. Long John Silver had a wooden
leg instead of a real one and a parrot which perched
on his shoulder screeching,

"pieces of eight... pieces of eight".

Two real pirates

Blackbeard

This wicked pirate started off with a very ordinary name, Edward Teach, and a very ordinary job of being a seaman. But in 1716 he became a pirate and grew a huge, jet-black beard. He liked his beard so much that he plaited it and tied ribbons in it.

He liked being wicked so much that he wore three pairs of pistols, a cutlass, lots of daggers and slow-burning fuses under his hat. It didn't do him any good though, because he was hunted down and killed, which was probably a good thing.

Grace O'Malley

Grace O'Malley, the Pirate Queen of Connaught, was born hundreds of years ago when all women wore long frocks. Grace became a pirate so that she could wear pirate clothes and sail the Seven Seas. She was very good at it and made lots of money robbing other ships.

Unfortunately some of the ships belonged to Queen Elizabeth I of England. Grace had to go to England to have her head chopped off, but amazingly, Queen Elizabeth seemed to like Grace and gave her a lace handkerchief instead. Perhaps she wished she could have been a pirate too, instead of just an ordinary queen.

Things to do

Message in a bottle

Imagine that you have been captured by pirates and then marooned on a deserted island. You have a few essential supplies such as a box of ship's biscuits and a bottle of grog, but you need to be rescued. Write a message which can be sealed up in a bottle and thrown into the sea.

Wanted Poster

Make your own **Wanted** poster by dressing your best friend up as a pirate (use old curtain rings for earrings, spotty hanky wrapped around head, false beard on chin etc.) and drawing a picture of them. Try inventing your own 'olde worlde' style of writing for the words on the poster.

Pirates' treasure map

To help pirates find treasure they always have a treasure map which is usually very, very old and difficult to follow. It is dipped in tea and torn around the edges, then rolled up and fastened with ribbon. Can you make your own treasure map?

Pirates' grog

T̶his is a drink which pirates make to keep them warm on deck. It also has plenty of vitamin C in it which stops them from getting scurvy.

For each pirate you need:
1 *lemon*
1 *tablespoon of brown sugar*
1 *pinch of powdered ginger*
1 *jug of hot water*

Directions

1 Cut the lemon in half and squeeze out the juice.
2 Put juice in jug and add sugar and ginger.
3 Add hot water and stir well.